W9-BKY-370

Children's Costumes

Children's Costumes

A treasure trove of amazingly
original designs – simple to make
and fun to wear

GILL DICKINSON

646.478
D 553 c

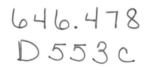

CHARTWELL
BOOKS, INC.

HARTFORD PUBLIC LIBRARY

A   QUINTET   BOOK

Published by Chartwell Books
A Division of Book Sales, Inc.
110 Enterprise Avenue
Secaucus, New Jersey 07094

This edition produced for sale in the U.S.A.,
its territories and dependencies only.

Copyright © 1993 Quintet Publishing Limited.
All rights reserved. No part of this publication may
be reproduced, stored in a retrieval system or
transmitted in any form or by any means,
electronic, mechanical, photocopying, recording
or otherwise, without the permission of the
copyright holder.

ISBN 1-55521-919-5

This book was designed and produced by
Quintet Publishing Limited
6 Blundell Street
London N7 9BH

Creative Director: Richard Dewing
Designer: Ian Hunt
Project Editor: Katie Preston
Editor: Jenny Millington
Photographers: Paul Forrester and Chas Wilder

Typeset in Great Britain by
Central Southern Typesetters, Eastbourne
Manufactured in Singapore by
Bright Arts (Singapore) Pte Ltd
Printed in Singapore by
Star Standard Industries (Pte) Ltd

Acknowledgements:
The models: Victoria Dewing, Spencer Dewing,
Jimmy Forrester, James Stuart, Lucy Stuart,
Richard van Nairn, Natasha Mytton Mills,
Alexandra Mytton Mills, Jade Lauren Lugay.
Artist's materials for photography supplied by
Daler Rowney. Leotards and catsuits from Tunics
Ltd. Ballet shoes from Rodwins Dancewear.

Contents

Introduction

People of all ages love dressing up – creating and wearing fancy dress is an exciting part of going to a special party or staging a play in the school holidays.

The fun starts at a very early age, so it's a good idea to keep a large box or chest especially for dressing-up materials, filling it with old clothes, shoes, pieces of fabric, beads and so on. All sorts of items can be pressed into service and a supply of cardboard and paper will also be very useful.

Most of the projects in this book are simple to make and require very little special skill. The costumes should be fun to create and to wear – this is more important than a perfect finish! All the ideas can be adapted to suit the materials available or the theme of a party – the main ingredient is always lots of imagination.

Starting a Project

The first decision is not always an easy one – which costume to make. The choice of character or object depends on the interests of the wearer as well as the theme of the occasion. Always look around the house to see what materials are available – old bits of fabric, Christmas cards and decorations, sequins, ribbons, wrapping paper, corrugated cardboard; they can all be useful, and will help you decide.

Some costumes can be planned well in advance of any parties or plays, and are a marvellous way of involving everyone, whatever their age. Even a complicated costume will usually need gluing, trimming and colouring, which even the smallest hands can manage, and everyone can use their imagination to the full.

Before you choose a project, ask yourself how much time and money you have to spare, and whether you want a traditional costume or a completely original one. Then use this book to inspire you.

Paper and Foil

Different papers can be a wonderful source of inspiration, and you should always keep odd pieces in the dressing-up box. Crepe paper is surprisingly strong, cheap to buy, and comes in a range of vibrant colours. The Clown project in this book shows how versatile crepe paper can be – use it for a huge bow tie or a Hawaiian shirt.

There are some beautiful foil-finish wrapping papers available in all sorts of patterns, and most kitchens contain at least one roll of baking foil.

PAPER AND FOIL

Plain coloured paper
Striped paper
Patterned wrapping paper
Crepe paper
Tissue paper
Ridged or dotted foil

Things You Will Need

The picture shows a selection of items that were used to make the costumes in this book. It is a good idea to collect bits and pieces like this in a box – you will be amazed at what you can find.

Food packaging comes in all shapes and sizes, such as yoghurt or margarine tubs, and can be sprayed different colours. Transparent containers can be used as they are, for the Robot costume for example.

Try to think of other uses for ordinary items. For instance, toilet roll tubes joined together could make a judge's wig or curly hair. Kitchen roll tubes could be used for the tubes on a space suit or a deep sea diver. Egg boxes could be cut up to make a monster mask.

BITS AND PIECES

Cardboard tubes from kitchen &
   toilet rolls
Corrugated cardboard
Plastic wall plugs
Cocktail sticks
Drinking straws
Paper plates, cups & bowls
Plastic knives & spoons
Coloured plastic tops from
   aerosols etc.
Plastic tubing from an electrical
   shop
Plastic food or chocolate
   containers
String
Leather laces
Egg boxes

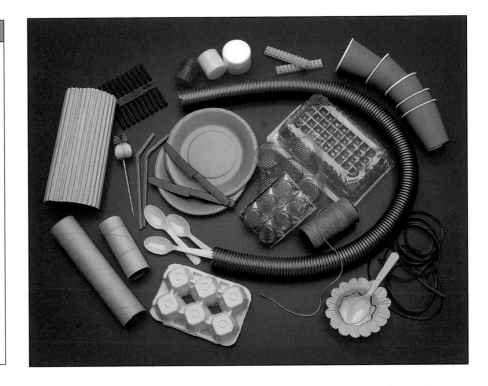

Pencils, Pens and Paints

All these things can be bought from art shops, and would make good presents for fancy dress makers of any age. Bear in mind that boxed crayons and gouache cost more than wax crayons and felt tip pens.

Instead of buying coloured paper, why not colour it yourself with marker pens, or by flicking paint on with an old toothbrush. A wax candle can be used to draw a design, which is then painted over with a wash of colour – the wax acts as a resist to stop the paint from settling. You can make stripes with masking tape, peeling it off after the paint has dried.

PENCILS, PENS AND PAINTS

Felt tip pens
Paint brushes
Pencils
Chalk pastels
Wax crayons
Coloured pencils
Gouache
Fabric paints
Poster paints

Trimmings

The secret is never to to throw anything away! Keep a box handy for the odd balloon or streamer left over from a party. The Christmas decoration box can be a great source of inspiration, not only for costumes with a Christmas theme. The Grandfather Clock project in this book uses Christmas baubles for handles and a sun for decoration. A piece of tinsel will liven up any costume, and ribbons and sequins are a must.

TRIMMINGS
Feathers
Ribbons
Tinsel
Christmas decorations
Streamers
Balloons
Sequins
Glitter
Self adhesive stars
Beads

Fabrics

Your local market is probably a good source of cheap fabric offcuts. You don't even have to be expert at sewing – fabrics can be glued or even stapled! Let the pattern and texture of the material inspire you – the net was used for the Fairy costume, the chamois leather for the Red Indian, and the spotted fabric for the Pirate.

FABRICS
Net – plain or with silver stars
Chamois leather
Patterned cotton & satin
Fake fur
Felt
Metallic material

Tools and Techniques

SEWING Most of the costumes in this book can be made without the use of a sewing machine, although machine-stitched seams are usually stronger than hand-sewn ones.

PAPIER MÂCHÉ This method of layering torn-up paper and a glue such as wallpaper paste or flour-and-water paste is very useful and great fun to do. Use it for masks or accessories.

GLUING Always choose a non-toxic glue, and make sure it is suitable for sticking the materials you are using.

PAINTING To paint large areas, buy the large bottles of poster paint – they are reasonably cheap and will cover most surfaces well.

PASTELS AND WAX CRAYONS A fixative spray is useful to stop the colours smudging.

FABRIC STENCILLING Small pots of fabric paint can be bought from most art shops. They have instructions on them, and most need fixing with heat, such as by ironing, to prevent the colours running.

STENCIL PAPER Proper stencil paper is thick and quite hard to cut. Layout paper is thinner and strong enough to use instead.

CARD AND CARDBOARD Card can be bought in various thicknesses from art shops, but supermarkets are a good source of free cardboard boxes in all sorts of thicknesses and qualities!

POLYBOARD This is a sort of sandwich of card and polystyrene which is very lightweight and can be cut with a craft knife after a little practice. Art shops usually stock various thicknesses.

DRESSMAKERS' PATTERN PAPER This thin paper can be bought from most department stores. It is made for dressmaking patterns and often has a grid printed on it.

WADDING This is used for stuffing toys etc., and can be bought from most department stores.

BROWN TAPE Wide brown parcel tape is excellent for strengthening the edges of cardboard boxes for costumes like the Birthday Present.

MASKING TAPE This will peel off shiny surfaces without damaging them, so it can be used for stencilling or making stripes with paint. It is also useful for joining the edges of paper together.

VELCRO This is not only a strong method of fastening edges together, but is also easier for small hands to cope with than buttons or hooks and eyes. Most department stores sell it in any length you require.

AEROSOL SPRAYS Paint and glue sprays must always be used with adult supervision and in a well-ventilated area. If possible, avoid using spray versions of paints and glues.

SCISSORS AND CRAFT KNIVES Use scissors in preference to craft knives when young children are helping. A cutting mat is almost essential when using a craft knife, to protect the surface you are cutting on. Always cut away from your free hand, and use a steel rule to give a straight edge.

HOW TO MAKE TEMPLATES

This book includes some patterns for parts of the costumes and these will need to be scaled up and made into templates. The patterns are printed on a squared grid. You will need a large sheet of plain paper, onto which you need to draw a grid of squares to the scaled-up size. For example if the scale is 1:8 then you will need to make your squares eight times as large as the ones in this book. Then copy the outline of the pattern onto your grid square by square. You will now have a full-size template to use for your costume.

Gather together all the equipment you need before starting a project.

Quick Costumes

Each chapter in this book ends with an idea for a Quick Costume. These are ideal for those last-minute demands for a fancy dress costume and can be made very quickly, often with materials that will be in the house already. Try to sum up a character in a few well-chosen items; make a judge's wig out of toilet-roll tubes joined together side by side, for example, or a rag doll's plaits out of skeins of wool. A monster could simply be some drinking straws stuck into a bathing hat. Use this list of suggestions as inspiration.

HATS These are very easy to make out of paper or card and can follow any number of themes: cowboy, nurse, Indian chief, schoolmaster, and so on. Make a Hawaiian hat with plastic fruit and a brightly coloured headsquare. Hats can also suggest more unusual things such as a cabbage, a butterfly or a wasp.

EARS These are great fun to wear and can conjure up an animal very simply and effectively. This book includes rabbit ears (see page 70) which could be adapted to all sorts of other creatures. Ears can also easily be made out of coloured paper.

BEAKS Look at some pictures of penguins, ducks, storks, parrots or pelicans to see the different shapes. Beaks are easy to make from stiff card, with elastic to hold them in place.

GLASSES Cut glasses shapes out of thin card and decorate with anything you like. You could make heart shaped ones for Valentine's Day; flowerpot shapes; ice creams.

1
TRADITIONAL CHARACTERS

Witch 12

Clown 16

Indian 20

Knave of Hearts 24

American Footballer 28

Witch

YOU WILL NEED

- Card to make stencils
- Black material for cloak
- String, pencil & drawing pin
- Silver glitter
- Glue
- Scissors & pinking shears
- Witch's hat or card to make one
- Plastic mice
- Plastic spiders
- Black bias binding
- Paint brush & white pencil
- Florists' wire

☞ This is a very simple costume to make and can be assembled without any sewing.

☞ The hat was bought, but could easily be made from card, using for example the Christmas Tree pattern (page 46) with a brim added.

☞ Old clothes could be worn under this costume, with wellingtons or black gym shoes if the wearer is going outdoors on Halloween.

☞ If you have an old pair of gloves, cut the fingers off and buy some false "talons" from a joke shop.

1 Cut out the cloak with pinking shears.

To cut out the cloak

Measure down the child's back from the nape of the neck. Double this figure, and make sure you buy enough fabric.

Fold the fabric in half. Draw an arc onto the fabric using a piece of string and a pencil attached to a drawing pin, as shown in the diagram. Cut across the corner to make the neck opening.

This method can also be used to make a full circle of fabric for a skirt to go under the cloak.

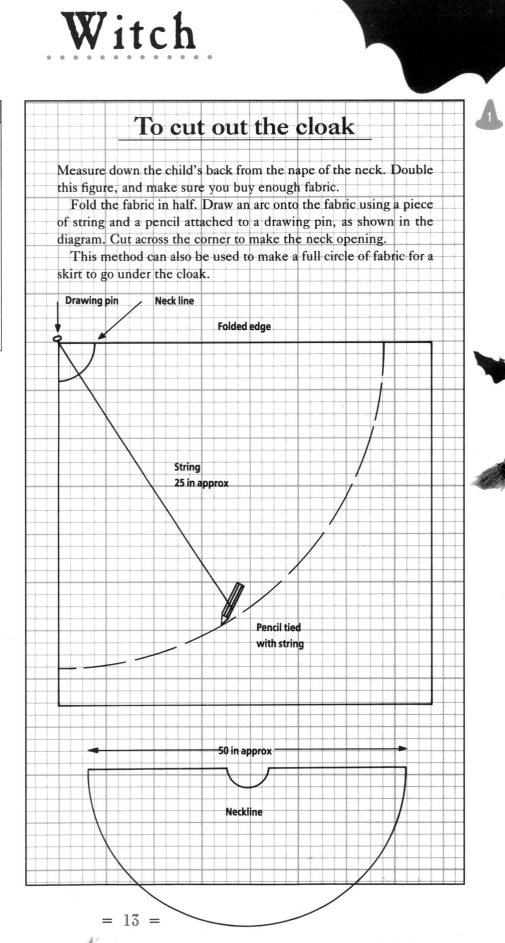

Drawing pin   Neck line

Folded edge

String
25 in approx

Pencil tied
with string

50 in approx

Neckline

Decorative shapes template

2 Cut out the star and moon templates and draw the shapes onto the fabric with white pencil.

3 Paint glue into the shapes very carefully.

4 Sprinkle glitter onto the glue until all the shapes are covered.

5 Brush any excess glitter carefully onto a sheet of paper and save for future use.

6 Sew or glue black bias binding onto the neck opening with long ends left to tie the cloak.

7 Trim the bottom edge of the cloak with pinking shears to the required length.

8 For the hat, draw the shapes, paint with glue and cover with glitter as for the cloak. Add some net with spiders attached, and a mouse to the brim of the hat.

9 Make a necklace of mice with wire.

HARTFORD PUBLIC LIBRARY

Clown

YOU WILL NEED

Coloured crepe paper
Sticky tape
Scissors
Shirring elastic
Thread
Tape for ends of the ruff
Wire
Glue
Self-adhesive dots
Clown party-hat
Striped socks
Sewing machine

☞ This costume will be easy to make if you are used to using dressmaking patterns.

☞ It can be machine or hand sewn.

☞ Make sure you cut the crepe paper across the grain for strength.

☞ Remember to leave a large gap in the back seam for the costume to be put on and taken off easily.

☞ This costume could also be made from harlequin printed fabric or satin.

☞ You could replace the patches with spots or stripes – the louder the better!

☞ Scale up the pattern to the size you need as described on page 9. The pattern illustrated would fit an average 4–5 year old. To make the pattern bigger, make the squares bigger than the recommended scale.

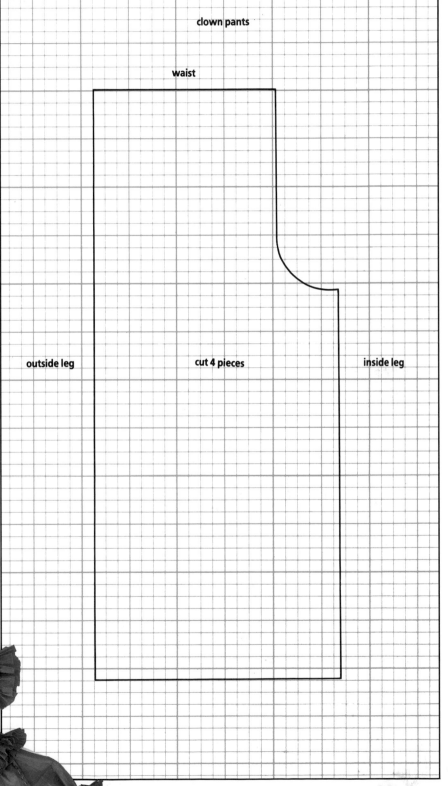

clown pants

waist

outside leg   cut 4 pieces   inside leg

1 large square = 1in (25mm)   *Scale* 1:5

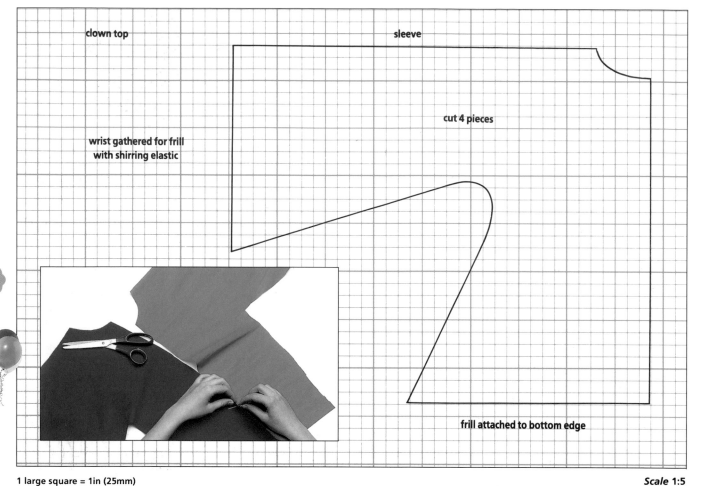

clown top

sleeve

cut 4 pieces

wrist gathered for frill
with shirring elastic

frill attached to bottom edge

1 large square = 1in (25mm)

Scale 1:5

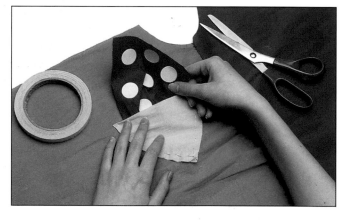

1 Cut out two pieces in each of two colours for the top of the costume. Stitch alternate coloured front pieces together down the middle. Repeat for the back.

2 For the ruff cut three coloured strips: yellow 28in × 5in (710mm × 127mm); blue 28in × 7in (710mm × 177mm); red 28in × 9in (710mm × 228mm). Place the blue strip on top of the red one, followed by the yellow strip, and sew a running stitch along the centre. Gather the strips

until about 15in (381mm) long, fold the ends over and stitch a tape tie to each end.

3 Stitch some patches onto the front of the jacket with shirring elastic or thick thread. Add a spotted handkerchief made from a square of red paper and self-adhesive dots.

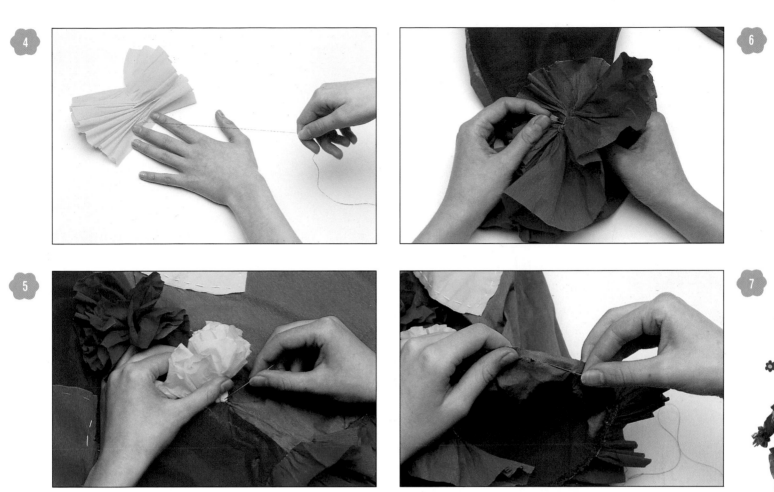

4 To make the pom-poms, cut some paper 20in × 7in (508mm × 177mm), stitch along the centre with a running stitch and gather together tightly.

5 Tie thread round the bottom of the pom-pom until it feels secure. Stitch the pom-poms to the middle of the jacket front. Sew the front and back top together with the right sides facing each other. Leave a 10in (254mm) gap at the back.

6 For the arm ruffle, cut a length of blue crepe paper 35in × 5in (890mm × 127mm), gather it 2in (50mm) from one end using shirring elastic until the ruffle is the right size. Stitch a ruffle to each sleeve.

7 From a strip of blue paper 120in × 3in (3048mm × 76mm), make a larger ruffle for the bottom edge of the jacket and stitch it into place. Cut two pieces each of two colours for the trousers, and stitch alternate colours together. Join the front and back of the trousers with right sides facing, then decorate with ruffles and patches as the top. Gather the waist with shirring elastic.

8 To decorate the hat, cut a red flower shape with a yellow centre and green leaves, and glue onto a length of wire. Push the wire through the top of the hat and secure with sticky tape. Add a pom-pom through a small hole in the front of the hat, securing the base with sticky tape.

North American Indian

YOU WILL NEED

Chamois leathers or other soft
  beige fabric to cover front and
  back from shoulder to knee
Beads & feathers
Scissors
Glue
Pencil
Fabric paint
Paint
Braid or ribbon for purse
Coloured paper
Necklaces
Toy bow & arrows
Plate

☞ Chamois leather can be bought quite cheaply from markets etc., and comes in a variety of shapes which add to the originality of the costume.

☞ Before you start, cut some fringing from the main pieces of fabric.

☞ Fringes could also be made from string glued onto a braid.

1 Choose suitable pieces of chamois leather for front and back and draw round a plate to make the shape of the neckline. Glue the front and back together at the shoulders and down the sides, leaving 8in (203mm) each side for the arm holes.

2 Cut some strips 3in (76mm) wide and make into fringing. Glue to the shoulders and sides of the tunic.

3 Make a triangle template and draw a pattern of triangles around the neckline.

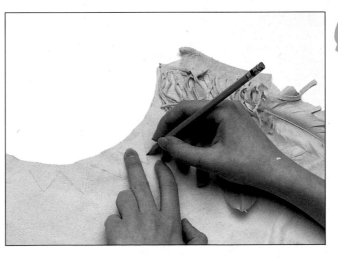

Decorative template

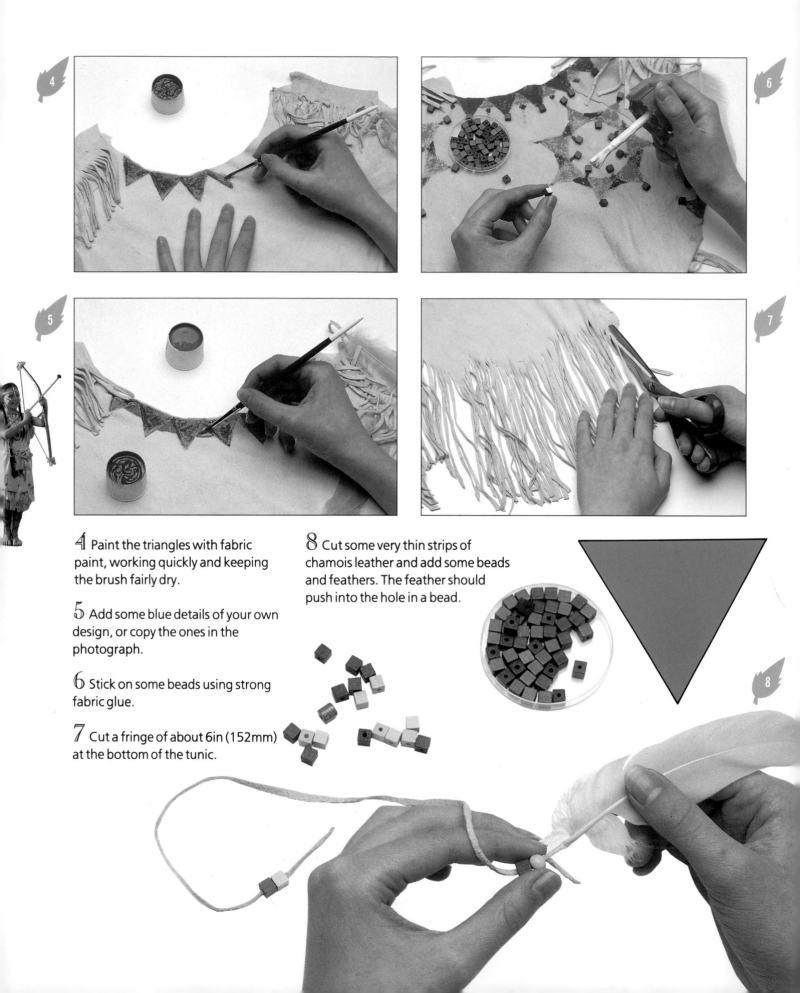

4 Paint the triangles with fabric paint, working quickly and keeping the brush fairly dry.

5 Add some blue details of your own design, or copy the ones in the photograph.

6 Stick on some beads using strong fabric glue.

7 Cut a fringe of about 6in (152mm) at the bottom of the tunic.

8 Cut some very thin strips of chamois leather and add some beads and feathers. The feather should push into the hole in a bead.

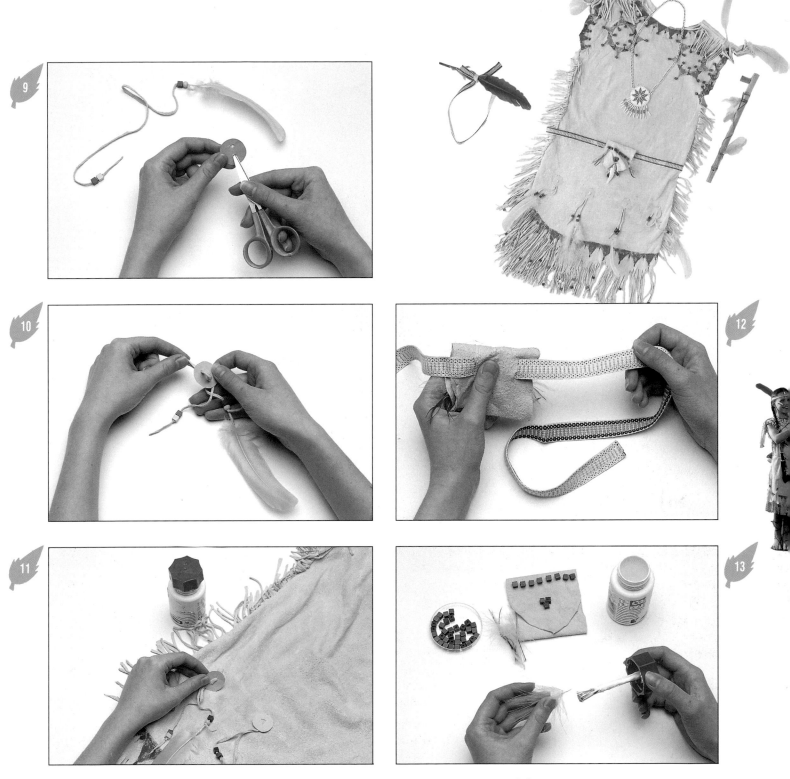

9 Make a circle of paper by drawing round a coin. Cut out and make two slits in the circle with scissors.

10 Pull the thong with the beads and feathers through the slits in the paper.

11 Glue the paper circle to the bottom of the tunic. To make the purse, cut a strip 10in × 3in (254mm × 76mm) and glue the sides together. Shape the top with scissors.

12 Make two slits in the back of the purse and thread a braid or ribbon through to tie around the waist.

13 Decorate the purse with beads and feathers. You could also make a head-dress with braid or ribbon decorated with beads and feathers.

Knave of Hearts

YOU WILL NEED

Paper large enough for the main
    section
Plate
Coloured papers for decoration
Sticky tape
Scissors or craft knife
Pencil
Glue

☞ You can wear this "sandwich-board" style costume over any clothing.

☞ This is an all-paper costume, so it is very cheap to make.

☞ Choose the brightest colours of paper you can find.

☞ Make up your own variation on the theme of hearts for the decoration.

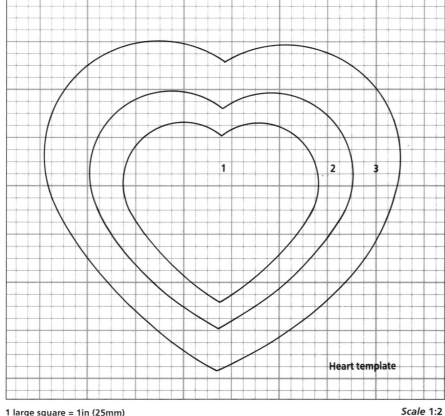

Heart template

1 large square = 1in (25mm)

Scale **1:2**

1 Join two sheets of coloured paper at the shoulder seams with sticky tape. Draw round a plate to make the shape of the neckline, and cut out. Make a 12in (304mm) cut down the back of the tunic.

2 Cut out heart shapes and long strips of contrasting coloured paper. Stick the heart shapes on top of each other as shown.

3 Glue the coloured strips along the edges of the tunic, making sure each side matches.

4 Add hearts and any other decorations to the costume.

5 Cut out the collar using the template, and make small cuts all round the inside edge so that it will fit the neck of the tunic more easily.

6 Decorate with hearts and diamonds.

7

9

8

7 Cut out the cuffs using the template and glue the separate sections together.

8 Decorate the cuffs with cut-out shapes.

9 Glue the final blue strip onto each cuff.

10 Cut out the crown shape and decorate with hearts. The crown is secured with sticky tape when finished.

10

American Footballer

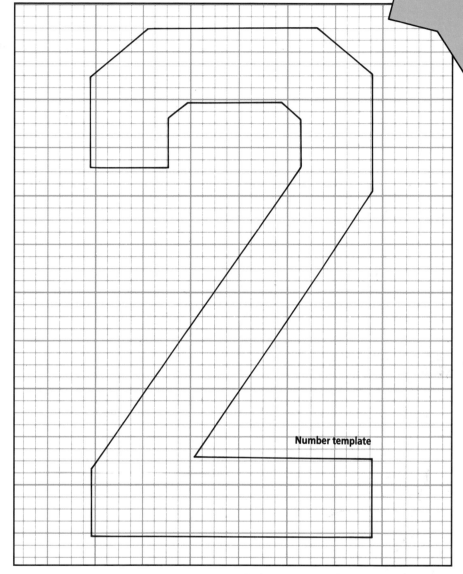

Number template

Scale 1:2   1 large square = 1in (25mm)

YOU WILL NEED

A cheap pair of leggings
White T shirt
Fabric paint
Stencil brush
Thin paper or layout paper
Balloon
Wadding
Pencil & paint brushes
Craft knife & hole punch
Papier mâché (wallpaper paste or
    flour-and-water paste &
    newspapers)
Bucket
Petroleum jelly or talcum powder
Electrical flex for helmet
Fuse wire or florists' wire
Masking tape & Blutack
Brown paper tape

☞ The helmet is time-consuming to make.

☞ The T shirt can be used again and again.

☞ For stencilling, always test a sample piece first to find the right consistency of paint. Keep the brush fairly dry and don't press too hard.

☞ A hairdryer will dry paint very quickly.

☞ Use the design and colours of your favourite football team.

Star template

1 Blow up the balloon large enough for the helmet. Make up a bucket full of thick paste and rip up newspapers into strips. Be sure to dust the balloon with talc before you start, or cover it with petroleum jelly, otherwise the papier mâché will stick. Cover the balloon with layers of newspaper strips soaked and painted with the paste. Allow each layer to dry before starting the next one.

2

5

3

6

2 After about four layers, and once all the paste is dry, burst the balloon. Draw the shape of the face opening onto the helmet and cut it out with a craft knife. Strengthen the cut edges with brown paper tape torn into small strips.

3 Draw your design onto the helmet in pencil.

4 Paint in the design. Finish all the painting before the next stage.

5 Make small holes in the top and sides of the helmet as shown. The holes must be small so that the flex fits tightly.

6 Fit the vertical piece of flex first. Try the helmet on the child to find the length you need, and take care not to cut it too short. Push the flex through the hole and secure with Blutack.

4

7 Fit the horizontal pieces of flex in the same way.

8 Where the pieces of flex cross, secure them together with fuse wire.

9 Make a stencil of your chosen number. Leave a wide margin of paper all round, as stencilling can be very messy!

10 Make a stencil of the star in the same way.

11 Decorate the T shirt using the stencils and fabric paint. Mask the stripes on the sleeves with masking tape. Always let one colour dry before starting the next one — usually the paint is fixed by ironing through some thin cotton fabric. It is best to put a sheet of paper inside the T shirt to keep the paint from soaking right through.

12 Make the shoulder and leg pads out of wadding. Double over the wadding and glue the edges together for extra thickness.

Pirate and Chinese Costume

YOU WILL NEED

Spotted material or a red
    headsquare
Earring
False moustache & eyelash glue to
    attach
Black paper
Elastic
Plastic parrot
Striped T shirt
Jeans

☞ Moustaches and eye patches can be bought from joke shops.
☞ The eye patch could be made from black paper and elastic.
☞ Borrow a large earring, or make one from an old curtain ring.

YOU WILL NEED

Card
Coloured paper
Bright coloured fabric
Crepe paper

☞ Make the hat using the instructions for the Firework (page 78) but a little more shallow in shape.
☞ Pleat a piece of coloured paper as a fan.
☞ Wrap two pieces of fabric around the body, crossing back and front.
☞ Wind a wide piece of crepe paper round the waist as a cummerbund.
☞ Wear pyjama bottoms or leggings.
☞ A boy could wear a false moustache.

2
FESTIVE COSTUMES

Easter Egg 34

Christmas Fairy 38

Christmas Pudding 42

Christmas Tree 46

Birthday Present 50

Easter Egg

YOU WILL NEED

- Coloured paper – yellow and white
- Card or polyboard
- Sticky tape & strong tape
- Scissors
- Craft knife & cutting mat
- Pencil
- Glue
- Webbing or tape for straps
- Tracing paper

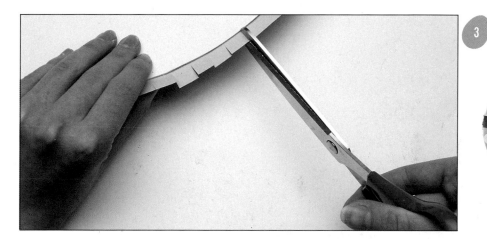

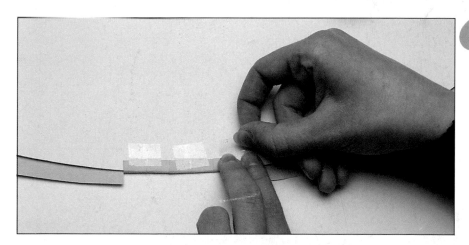

☞ Easy and cheap to make – children of any age can help.

☞ Measure the child from below the chin to the knees for the length of the egg.

☞ You can decorate the egg shape in any way you please, using bows, beads, sequins, pretty wrapping paper, even tinfoil.

☞ Any type of hat could go with this costume – a nest made out of straw, an Easter bonnet (page 54), even a little basket tied under the chin with ribbon.

1 Draw an egg shape the right size for your costume onto card or polyboard. You can create an egg shape by using two different sized plates; draw round the smaller one to form the top of the egg, use the larger plate for the bottom of the egg, and join the two with a curved line.

2 Cut out the egg shape with scissors or a craft knife.

3 From yellow paper, cut another egg shape about 1in (25mm) larger than the first. Place it under the card egg and snip the edge all the way round.

4 Turn back the edge of the yellow paper over the card and fix with sticky tape.

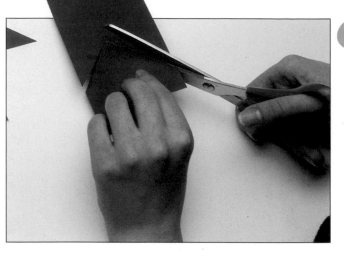

5 Cut some circles of white or coloured paper and glue them onto the front of the egg.

6 Cut strips of contrasting coloured paper, wrap across the egg and glue to the underside.

7 Take another strip of paper and fold it into the shape of a bow. Fix the ends with sticky tape at the back.

8 Cut two short strips for the tails and snip the ends with scissors.

9 Stick the tails to the bow then glue the whole bow to the centre of the egg. Attach two lengths of webbing to the top of the egg. Place the straps over the shoulders, cross over the back and tie at the waist.

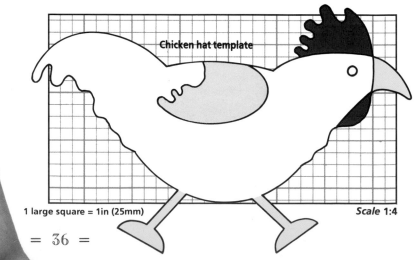

Chicken hat template

1 large square = 1in (25mm)

Scale 1:4

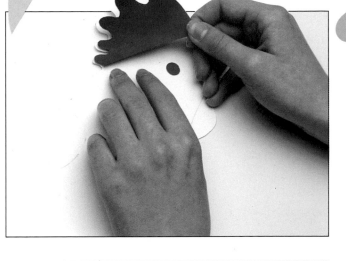

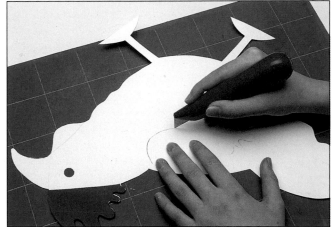

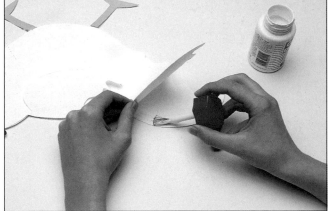

10 To make the hat, scale up the chicken from the template onto tracing paper. Transfer the drawing onto paper, making two copies, and cut them both out with scissors.

11 Draw round the chicken's comb onto red paper and cut out two copies. Do the same for beaks, feet (in yellow) and eyes (in blue).

12 Glue each piece carefully into position on the two chickens.

13 Cut out the wing on each chicken.

14 Glue the two chickens together along the top edge, leaving the bottom open to fit onto the head as a hat. Secure the hat with hair clips.

Christmas Fairy

YOU WILL NEED

Three layers of net – two plain, one
    with stars
Diamanté
Glue
Card for template
Silver tinsel & glitter
Dowelling
Plain plastic hair band
Silver spray paint
Three wire coathangers
Silver fabric
Leotard, shoes & tights
Florists' wire
Waistband of elastic
Needle & thread
Scissors & craft knife
Wadding
Pencil
Safety pins

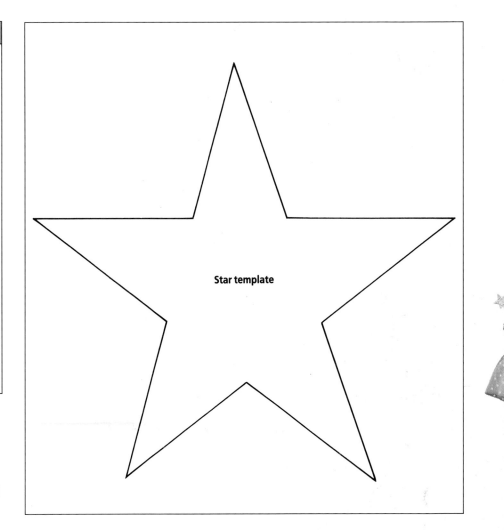

Star template

☞ A special costume for a little girl
– well worth the extra time it takes
to make.
☞ A white leotard and ballet shoes
would look really pretty but it would
be easy to find cheaper substitutes.
☞ The wings are attached to the
back of the leotard with safety pins
through wadding onto the leotard
straps.

1 Make the skirt by stitching
together three layers of net into
tubes of the required length. Put the
tubes together and stitch a running
stitch along one edge. Gather the
material up and sew into the elastic
waistband. Decorate the outer layer
with diamanté. Put tinsel around the
waist and neckline for extra sparkle.

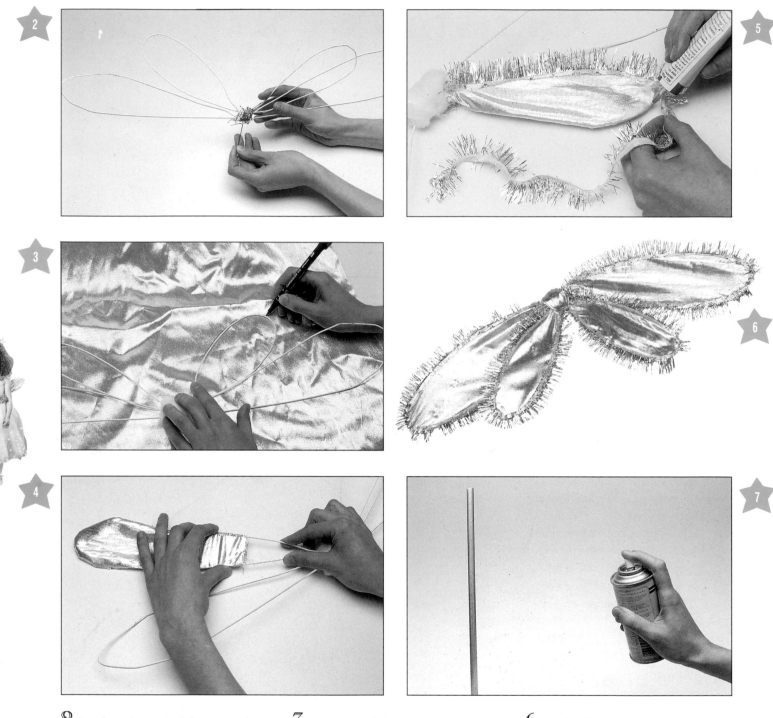

2 For the wings, straighten out the wire coathangers and bend the wire into wing shapes, two large and two smaller ones. Wire them together in pairs, then join the pairs in the centre using wadding and wire.

3 Draw round the wings onto silver fabric and cut out.

4 Stitch two pieces of fabric together, turn inside out and slip onto wire wings.

5 Glue some tinsel round the edge of each wing.

6 Finish off with a strip of silver fabric glued over the wadding in the centre.

7 To make the wand, spray or paint a 18in (457mm) piece of dowel silver.

8 Draw round the star template onto stiff card.

9 Cut out the star with a craft knife.

10 Cover the star on one side with glue. Sprinkle on silver glitter and shake off excess onto a spare piece of paper. The star could of course be sprayed silver instead.

11 Stick the star to the end of the silver dowel using tape.

12 To make the head-dress, cover a plastic hair band with silver tinsel.

13 Make a star in the same way as for the wand and attach it to the front of the head-dress with wire.

Christmas Pudding

YOU WILL NEED

Papier mâché: wallpaper paste or
   flour-and-water paste,
   newspapers & a bucket
Giant balloon
Bowl to rest balloon on between
   layers of papier mâché
Petroleum jelly or talcum powder
Poster paints & brushes
Heavy green paper for holly leaves
Polystyrene balls for berries
Florists' wire
Felt tip pen
Card for templates
Scissors & craft knife
Stapler
Hair grips
Pencil
Tinsel

Tips for making papier mâché

☞ The strips of newspaper are better torn than cut to shape.

☞ Always tear the strips in the same direction from the newspapers.

☞ Use different coloured paper to distinguish between layers, or lay the newspaper strips in alternating directions.

☞ Always allow each layer to dry completely before putting on the next one.

☞ When drying, don't put the papier mâché in front of a heater or radiator because the balloon will expand and crack the paper shell.

☞ One layer takes about 30–40 minutes to dry, and the Christmas Pudding costume needs six or seven layers for strength.

1 Blow up the giant balloon and mark a circle about 7in (178mm) in diameter for the neck hole. Opposite the neck, mark another circle about 30in (762mm) in diameter for the legs.

2 Cover the balloon with petroleum jelly or talcum powder to stop the papier mâché from sticking.

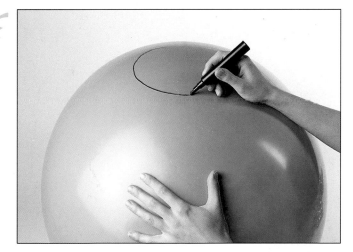

3 Mix a bucket full of thick paste and tear up lots of old newspapers into strips.

4 Dip the strips of newspaper into the paste.

5 Begin to cover the body of the balloon with the papier mâché, building up gradually layer by layer and allowing each layer to dry thoroughly. Six layers will probably be strong enough.

6 Burst the balloon with a pin. Draw the shape of the white sauce onto the top of the pudding in pencil.

7 Paint the sauce at the top white.

8 Paint the lower part of the pudding in a mixture of browns, with dabs of red and black to represent cherries and raisins etc.

9 Cut two arm holes in the sides with a sharp craft knife.

Holly leaf template

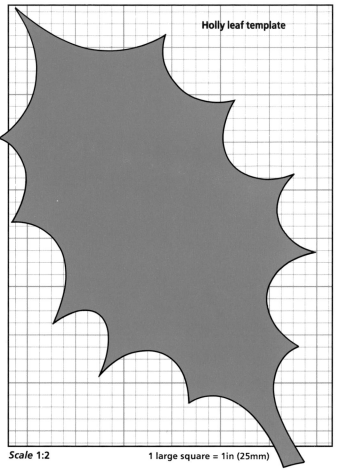

Scale **1:2**   1 large square = 1in (25mm)

10 Draw round the holly leaf template onto stiff green paper. Cut out the leaves and score and fold each one in half down the middle.

11 Fix each polystyrene ball to a piece of wire to make the berries.

12 Paint the berries red.

13 Arrange the holly leaves and berries together and fix with a staple or two. Secure on the wearer's head with hair grips.

Christmas Tree

YOU WILL NEED

Paper or thin card for hat
Two shades of green crepe paper
A selection of Christmas tree
    ornaments
Tinsel
Shirring elastic
Needle & thread
Ribbon
Tartan ribbon
Green net
Star for top of hat
Scissors
Florists' wire
Rolled elastic for hat strap
Stapler
Sticky tape
Pencil

☞ This is a cheap and simple costume, although it is quite time-consuming to make.

☞ Many of the items can be found in the Christmas decoration box and the sewing box.

☞ First you will need to cut the paper and net to size. For the top: light green paper 60in × 14in (1524mm × 355mm); dark green paper 60in × 8in (1524mm × 203mm); green net 60in × 15in (1524mm × 381mm).

For the skirt: light green paper 90in × 17in (2286mm × 431mm); dark green paper 90in × 11in (2286mm × 279mm); green net 75in × 19in (1905mm × 482mm).

1 For the top, fold the crepe paper and cut one end into points as shown.

2 Cut similar points into one edge of the net.

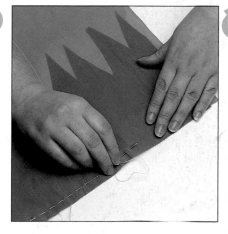

3 Place the paper on top of the net to make three layers as shown in the photograph. Sew a running stitch along the top edge.

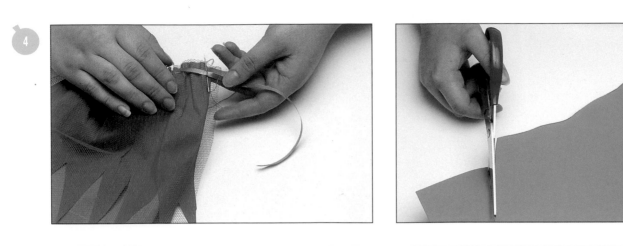

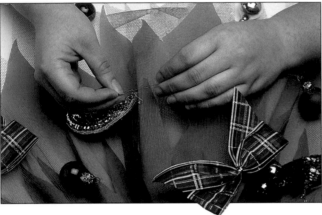

4 Gather the stitching up until the neck opening measures about 24in (609mm) and reinforce with an extra row of hand or machine stitching. Sew a ribbon onto each end to serve as ties. Make up the skirt in the same way, following steps 1–4.

5 Add Christmas ornaments and bows to both top and skirt using florists' wire.

6 To make the hat, copy the template shape onto the green card and cut out with scissors.

7 Roll the card into a cone shape and staple together.

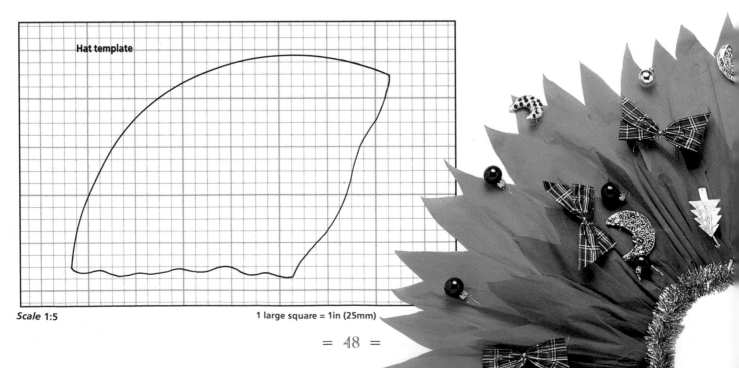

Hat template

Scale 1:5   1 large square = 1in (25mm)

8 Cut three pieces of net 48in × 8in (1219mm × 203mm), 48in × 7in (1219mm × 177mm) and 32in × 6in (812mm × 152mm). Trim each piece to points and gather one edge with shirring elastic.

9 Cut three strips of crepe paper 40in × 7in (1016mm × 177mm), 30in × 6in (762mm × 152mm) and 25in × 6in (635mm × 152mm). Cut out points and gather up.

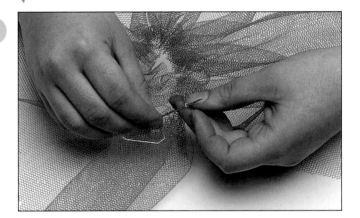

10 Cover the cardboard cone with alternate layers of crepe paper and net, securing each piece with sticky tape.

11 Decorate the hat with Christmas ornaments.

12 Knot the length of rolled elastic and staple it onto the hat as a chin strap.

Birthday Present

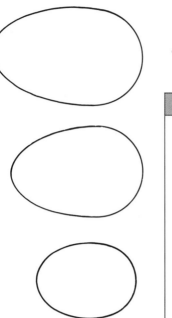

Dots template

YOU WILL NEED

A cardboard box to fit child
Sticky tape & double-sided tape
Wide sticky tape or parcel tape
Scissors & craft knife
Green ribbon
Red card for label
String
Florists' wire
Black spotted paper
Hole punch
Pencil

☞ This costume was made for a 6–8 year old.
☞ You could use old wallpaper, wrapping paper or even plain lining paper decorated with paints and crayons.
☞ The costume could just as easily be a Christmas present, with the addition of some Christmas decorations and tinsel.

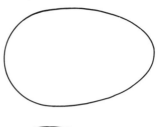

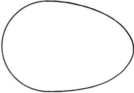

1 Strengthen the edges of the box with wide sticky tape. Cut the bottom of the box off.

2 Draw a 7in (177mm) diameter circle on the top of the box. Cut out the circle with a craft knife. Draw and cut out an arm hole on each side of the box. The holes should be about 6in (152mm) deep × 4in (101mm) wide, and about 5in (127mm) from the top of the box.

3 Cover the box with your chosen patterned paper. The paper can cover the neck and arm holes.

4 Pierce the paper in the centre of the neck and arm holes, then cut it back to the edge in a series of points.

5 Fold the points in through the hole and secure with sticky tape to make a neat edge.

6 Make a large bow from ribbon. The paper ribbon used here needs to be unravelled before you use it. Seal the centre of the bow with sticky tape.

7 Wrap a small strip of matching ribbon round the centre of the bow to hide the tape.

8 Run some ribbon round the box in both directions and secure inside the neck and arm holes with sticky tape. Add the bow using florists' wire.

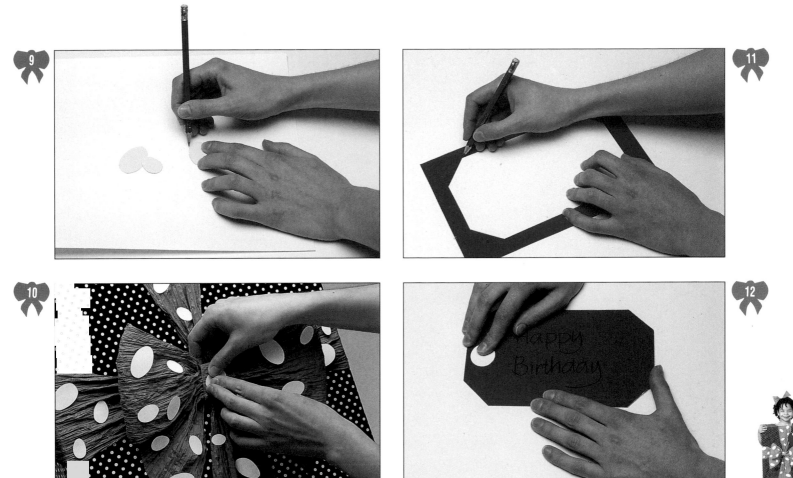

Scale 1:4

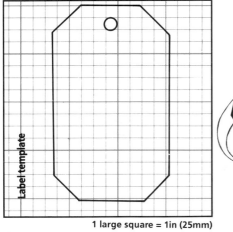

Label template

1 large square = 1in (25mm)

9 Make a dot template and draw round it onto white card to make the dots for the ribbon.

10 Stick the dots to the ribbon with double-sided tape.

11 Make the label by using the template.

12 Add a circle of white paper at one end and punch a hole through it.

13 Thread some string through the hole and tie the label to the present. Write a suitable message on the label.

Easter Bonnet

YOU WILL NEED

Coloured papers
Straws
Scissors
Glue
Sticky tape
Pencil

☞ Cut a large circle of paper for the brim of the hat.

☞ In the centre, cut a hole large enough to fit the child's head.

☞ Cut some flower shapes from coloured paper. Several layers of different colours could be used for each one.

☞ Push a straw through the middle of each flower and secure with sticky tape.

☞ Cut out some green paper leaves with long stems.

☞ Arrange the flowers and leaves in a bunch and tape to the brim of the hat.

☞ Decorate the hat with egg shapes or dots.

3
ANIMALS AND PLANTS

Sunflower 56

Leopard 60

Zebra 64

Cat Mask 66

Sunflower

YOU WILL NEED

Card or polyboard
Scissors & craft knife
Crepe paper in yellow, green & black
Black beads
Glue
Fabric tape
Card
Double-sided tape
Needle & thread
Yellow leotard
Green tights
Pencil

☞ This costume was made for a 4–7 year old.

☞ The sunflower face could be replaced by a leafy hat like the Pineapple (see page 96) or even just a big yellow bow if you are short of time.

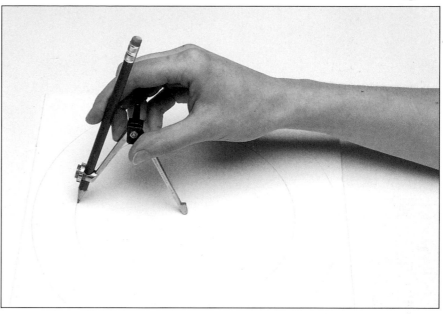

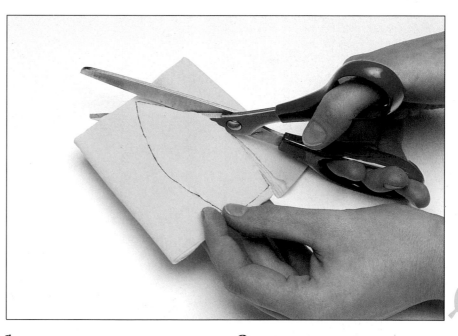

1 To make the "face" of the sunflower, draw a 9in (228mm) diameter circle on card or polyboard with a second circle in the middle to form a ring about 2in (50mm) wide. Cut out with a craft knife.

2 Use the templates to mark out three sizes of face petals from the yellow crepe paper and cut them out with scissors.

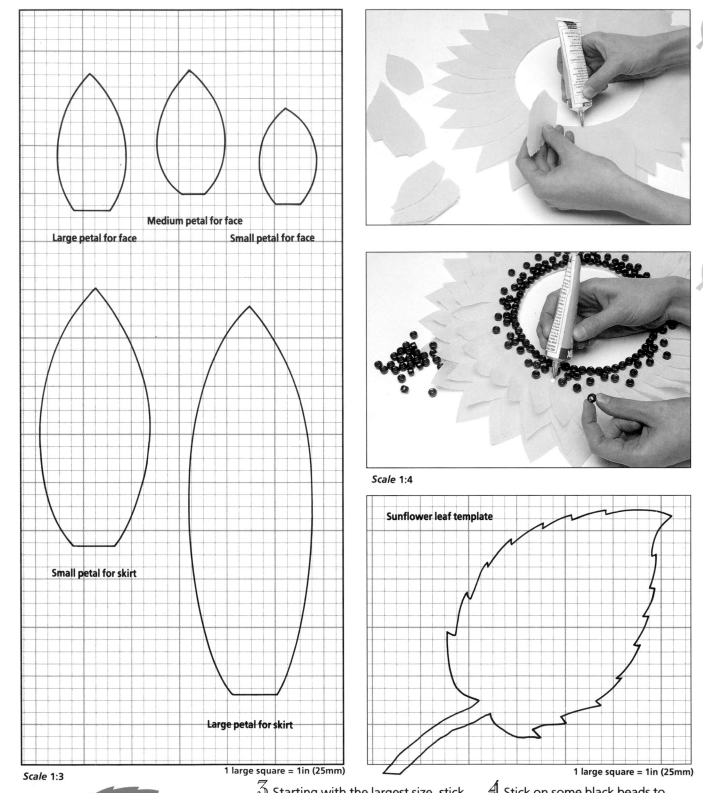

Medium petal for face

Large petal for face

Small petal for face

Small petal for skirt

Large petal for skirt

Scale 1:3

1 large square = 1in (25mm)

Sunflower leaf template

Scale 1:4

1 large square = 1in (25mm)

3 Starting with the largest size, stick the petals round the ring of card, with each layer overlapping the last slightly and the petals growing smaller.

4 Stick on some black beads to represent the sunflower seeds.

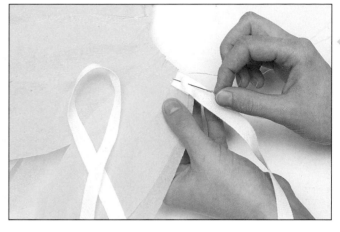

5 Turn the card over and attach some fabric tapes to act as ties.

6 For the skirt, cut out about 45 large yellow petals and about 45 smaller ones. Overlap the large petals slightly and sew them together.

7 Place the smaller petals over the larger ones and sew them into position.

8 Sew some fabric tape to each end of the row of petals to act as a tie. Cut a long piece of black crepe paper and fold it up to a width of about 2in (50mm). Stick this to the top of the skirt with double-sided tape, leaving enough to tie together at the back (see main photograph).

9 Using the template, cut three leaves and stick them to the leotard with double-sided tape.

Leopard

YOU WILL NEED

- Scaled-up pattern (see page 9 for instructions)
- Leopardskin-printed material
- Fur fabric
- Sewing machine
- Pins, thread & safety pins
- Scissors & pinking shears
- Velcro
- Fabric glue
- Elastic
- Wadding
- Black paper & eyelash glue for whiskers
- A pair of non-slip socks

☞ This costume could be stitched by hand, but it would take much longer.

☞ Trimming edges with pinking shears saves having to hem them to prevent fraying.

☞ The costume consists of an all-in-one suit, a hat, feet and mittens.

☞ Whiskers can be cut from black paper and stuck to the face with eyelash glue.

1 For the suit, cut out the pieces in the leopardskin fabric according to the pattern, and sew up the centre front and centre back seams, remembering to leave a 12in (304mm) opening in the back. You should also leave an opening for the tail. Stitch the side seams and trim the edges with pinking shears.

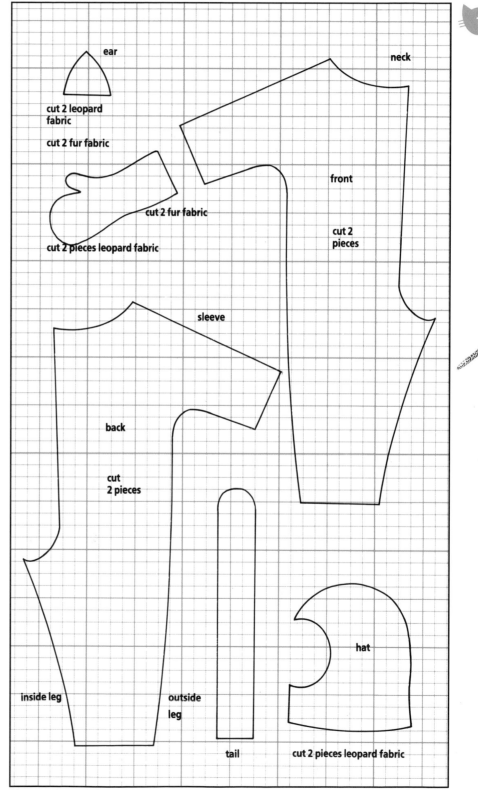

ear
cut 2 leopard fabric
cut 2 fur fabric

neck

cut 2 fur fabric

cut 2 pieces leopard fabric

front

cut 2 pieces

sleeve

back

cut 2 pieces

inside leg

outside leg

tail

hat

cut 2 pieces leopard fabric

1 large square = 1in (25mm)

Scale 1:8

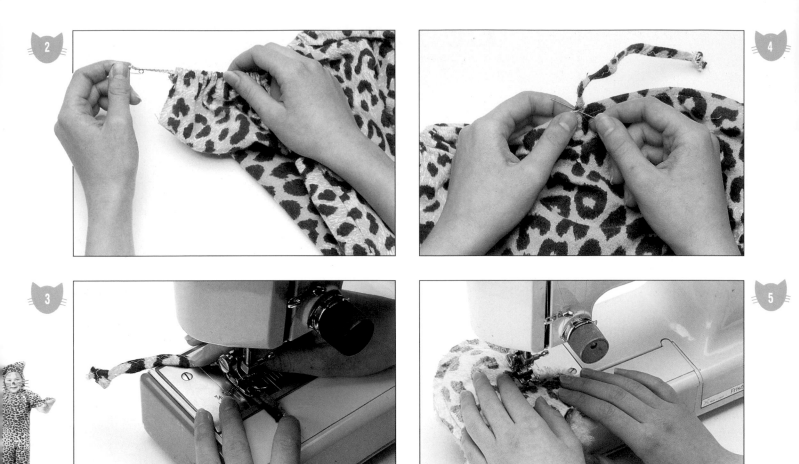

2 Make a ¾in (19mm) hem round the neckline and stitch by hand or machine, leaving a gap for the elastic. Thread the elastic through using a closed safety pin attached to the end.

3 Cut two strips of fabric for the ties 8in × 1in (203mm × 25mm) and fold them in half along their length. Machine stitch, knotting the ends to prevent fraying.

4 Sew one strip onto each side of the neckline of the suit by hand.

5 For the mittens, cut two pieces in leopardskin and two in fur fabric. Sew a piece of fur fabric to a piece of leopardskin fabric with the right sides together.

6 To make the hat, cut out the pieces according to the pattern, and machine the two side pieces to the centre section. Try the hat on the child and mark where the ears are to go, then make a small slit for each

ear. The ears are made of fur fabric and leopardskin fabric like the mittens, then stuffed with wadding. They can be pinned and sewn into position with the main part of the hat inside-out.

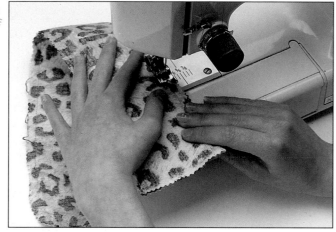

9 Turn the tail right-side out and stuff with wadding. Stitch it into position on the suit.

10 For the feet, use a pair of non-slip socks. Glue a piece of leopardskin fabric onto the top of each sock.

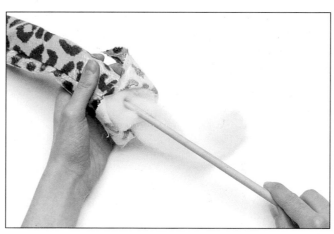

7 Sew or stick some velcro onto the neck of the hat for fastening at the front.

8 Cut out the tail according to the pattern and sew the pieces together with their right sides facing.

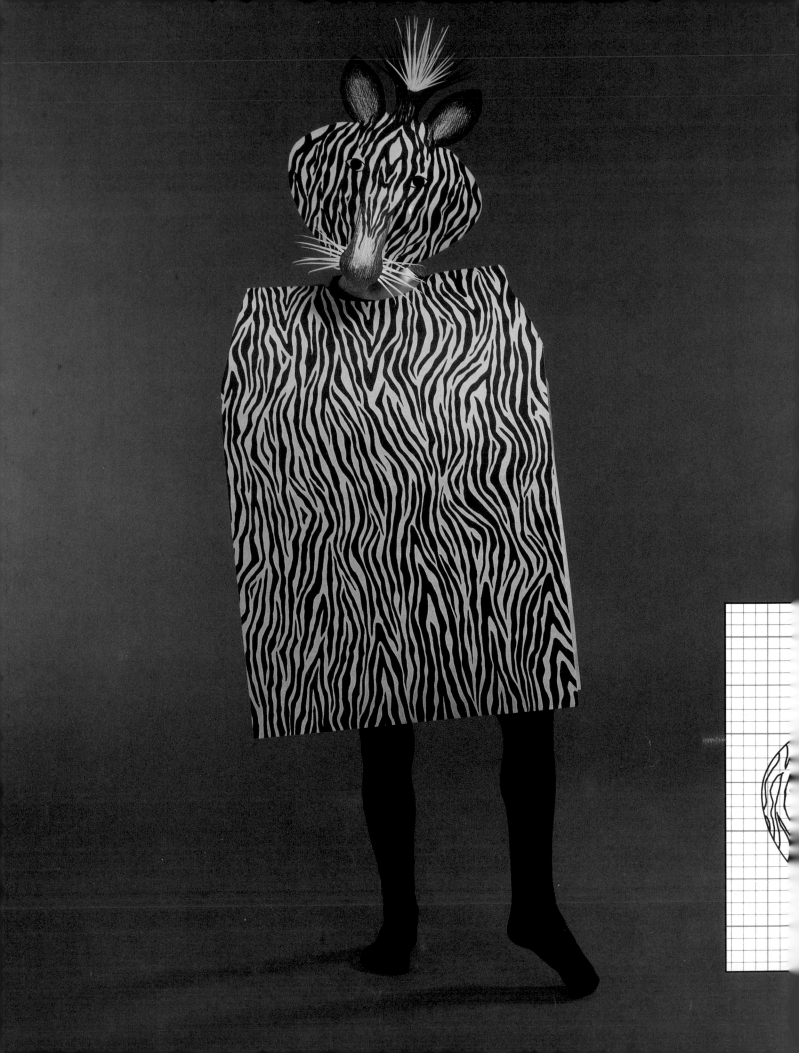

Zebra

YOU WILL NEED

Tracing paper
Scissors & craft knife
Zebra pattern paper
Plain heavy paper or card
Elastic
Sticky tape
Black felt tip pen or crayon
Ruler
Plate
Pencil

☞ This is an all-paper costume that a child could make quite easily.

☞ It was inspired by some recycled paper which was part of a range of animal prints – they would all have been fun to make.

☞ This basic idea could be adapted to all sorts of animals – tigers or dalmations for instance – and could be the basis of costumes for a play.

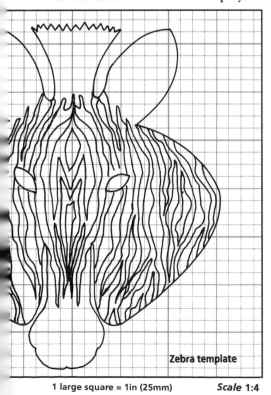

Zebra template

1 large square = 1in (25mm)   *Scale* 1:4

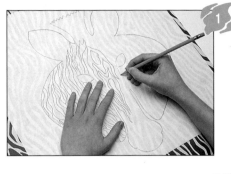

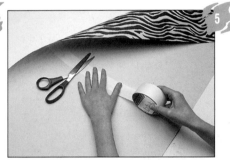

1 Use the template to trace off the mask by placing some tracing paper over the zebra-patterned paper. Fill in the lines you have traced off with pencil shading.

2 Transfer the mask to the heavy paper or card by turning the tracing over, placing it face-down on the card and rubbing the back with a coin. Fill in the lines on the card with black pen.

3 Cut out the mask, then cut some thin whiskers from plain white paper and glue into position. Remember to

cut along the sides of the nose piece and also to make two eye holes.

4 Turn the mask over and tape some elastic to the back.

5 Place two sheets of zebra pattern paper side by side and stick them together firmly on the back with sticky tape.

6 Draw round a plate to make the neckline and cut out the neck hole. Cut a 12in (304mm) slit down the middle of the back so that the tunic can fit over the head.

Cat Mask

YOU WILL NEED

White paper
Pencil
Paint & paint brush, coloured pencils
  or crayons
Sticky tape
Elastic
Scissors
Glue

☞ A black-and-white cat would be very easy to make using black paper and white paint.
☞ Make a tail out of paper, or fabric stuffed with wadding like the Leopard.
☞ Copy your favourite cat!
☞ Wear masks with contrasting T-shirt and leggings.

1 Using the template, draw out the mask shape onto the paper .

Scale **1:3**

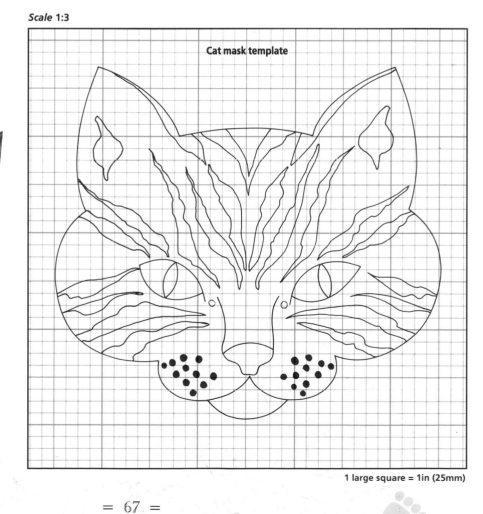

Cat mask template

1 large square = 1in (25mm)

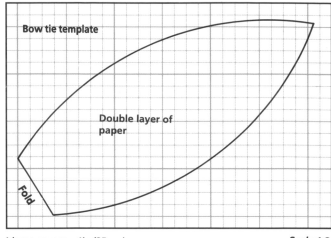

Bow tie template

Double layer of paper

Fold

1 large square = 1in (25mm)   *Scale* **1:3**

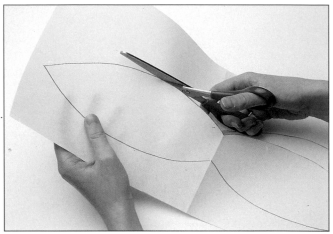

2 Draw and colour in the cat's markings.

3 Cut out some thin whiskers from white paper and stick them onto the mask. Cut out the eye holes marked on the template.

4 To make the bow tie, use the template to cut out the shape from white paper.

5 Draw and colour in the cat markings to match the mask. The ends can be left blank.

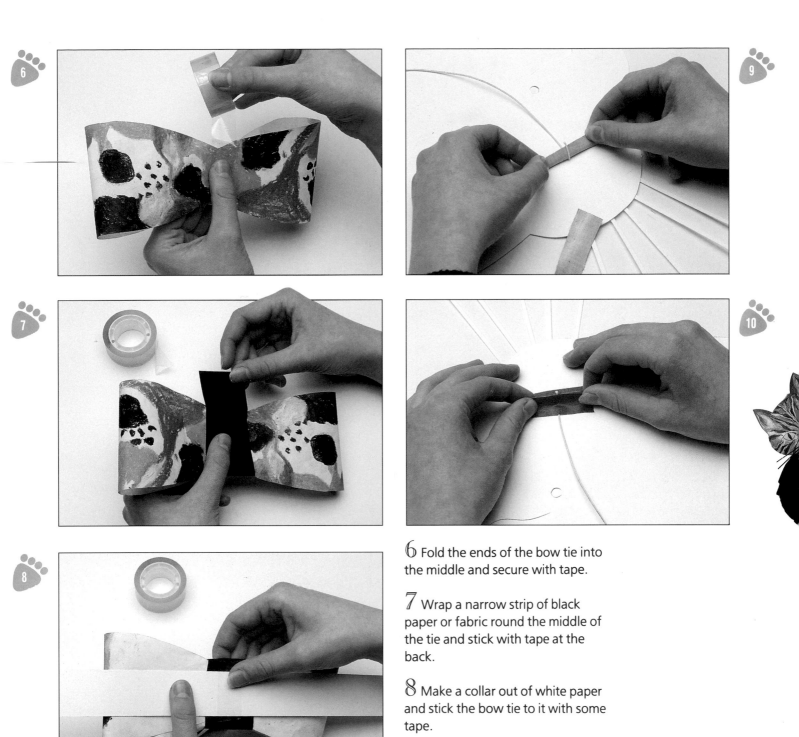

6 Fold the ends of the bow tie into the middle and secure with tape.

7 Wrap a narrow strip of black paper or fabric round the middle of the tie and stick with tape at the back.

8 Make a collar out of white paper and stick the bow tie to it with some tape.

9 Fix some elastic to the back of the mask with strong sticky tape.

10 Then stick another piece of tape onto the other side of the elastic so they butt together.

Rabbit Ears

YOU WILL NEED

Alice band
Felt – grey & white
Glue
Scissors
Cotton wool or wadding
Paper
Eyelash glue

☞ Cover an alice band with felt, gluing the edges and the ends down securely.

☞ Cut four ear-shaped pieces of grey felt and two smaller white pieces to make the insides of the ears.

☞ Glue each white piece to a grey piece of felt, then glue the pairs of grey pieces together, leaving a big enough opening to stuff with wadding or cotton wool.

☞ Glue the ends of the ears round the alice band and hold them in position until the glue has taken.

☞ Cut some thin whiskers from white paper and stick to the face with eyelash glue.

4
UNUSUAL
OBJECTS

Grandfather Clock 72

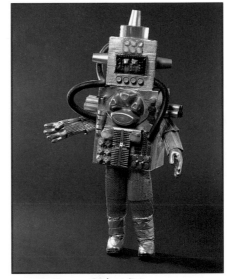

Robot 74

Firework 78

Teapot 82

YOU WILL NEED

3 cardboard boxes
Brown & white paint
Christmas bauble and sun face for
   decoration
Gold & white card
White paper
Black felt tip pen
Scissors & craft knife
Sticky tape
Glue & double-sided tape

☞ This costume is cheap and easy to make but looks very impressive! The painting can be quite messy, so it's a good idea to lay out lots of newspaper and wear an apron.

☞ The sun face used here was a Christmas decoration, but almost any motif will do. Some real grandfather clocks have flowers or moons, etc.

☞ The clock could have arm holes but looks better without them – finger-holes could be cut in the sides to hold the boxes straight.

☞ You will need a helper to fit and adjust the top section.

Grandfather Clock

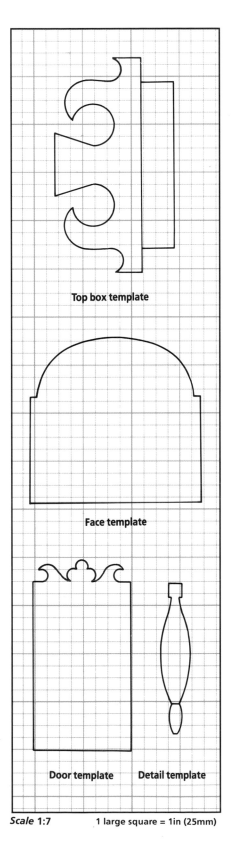

Top box template

Face template

Door template   **Detail template**

Scale **1:7**   1 large square = 1in (25mm)

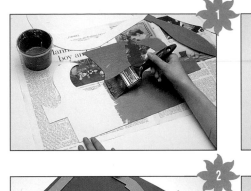

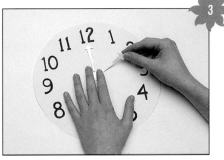

1 Choose two long boxes and one smaller one for the head. Strengthen the edges with tape and push the end flaps inside. Paint the boxes brown, and push one long box inside the other to make the main body. Trace the templates onto card and cut out the shapes with a craft knife. Paint all these pieces a lighter brown.

2 Stick the door shape onto the smaller box, make a small hole and push in a Christmas bauble for a doorknob. Slide the curly moulding inside the front of the box and secure it with tape.

3 Cut out a 9in (228mm) diameter circle of white paper and draw on the clock face numbers in black felt tip pen. Cut out clock hands from gold paper and glue them to the clock face.

4 Glue the face onto the front of the clock. Cut some eye holes.

5 Stick the side mouldings to the top of the clock with sticky tape. Glue the sun face down.

6 Glue the larger door shape to the front of the clock body and add a bauble for a doorknob.

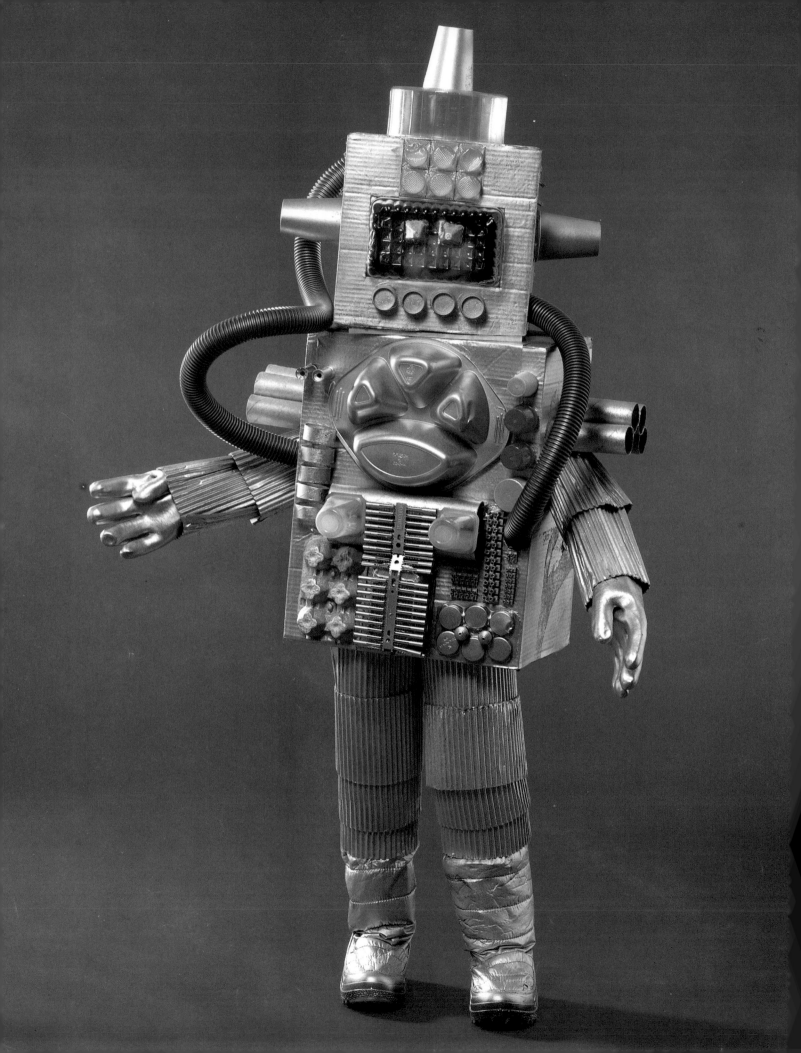

Robot

YOU WILL NEED

- 2 cardboard boxes
- Egg boxes
- Paper cups
- Toilet roll tubes
- Plastic aerosol tops, clear plastic containers etc.
- Corrugated tubes, wires etc.
- Corrugated cardboard
- Stapler
- Sticky tape, brown parcel tape & masking tape
- Craft knife
- Silver spray paint
- Glue
- Lots of old newspapers
- Wellingtons or old boots
- Rubber gloves

☞ Start collecting bits and pieces for this costume well in advance. An electrical shop that does repairs will be a good source for lengths of corrugated tubing such as old vacuum cleaner hose, wire, etc.

☞ Always spray paint in a really well-ventilated place, preferably outdoors.

☞ Remember to provide plenty of ventilation holes in the top of this costume – it can get quite hot inside!

1 Find a cardboard box big enough for the body of the wearer and strengthen the edges with parcel tape. Do the same with a smaller box for the head.

   Cut a rectangle from the bottom of the larger box, leaving a margin of about ½–1in (12–25mm) for strength.

2 Cut a circle from the top of the larger box that is big enough for the child's head. Cut arm holes in the sides too.

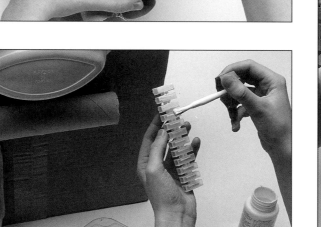

3 Join four toilet-roll rubes together side-by-side with sticky tape at both ends. Repeat for the other side of the costume.

4 Fix a set of tubes to the top of each arm hole with sticky tape or parcel tape.

5 Arrange your collection of tubes, wires and egg boxes on the front of the robot body. Make sure they are all glued or stapled firmly in place.

6 Mask any areas that are not to be sprayed silver with newspaper and masking tape. Spray the whole box silver, preferably out of doors, and allow it to dry.

7 Pull off the newspaper masks.

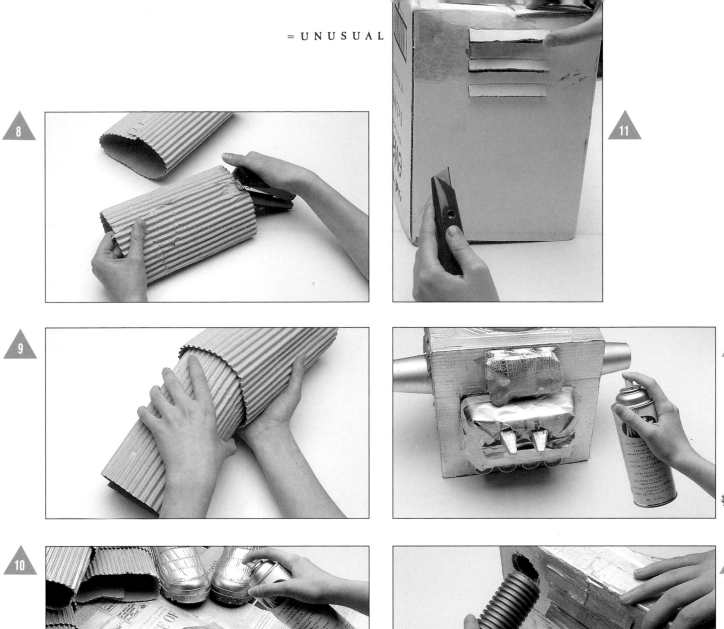

8 Measure the length of the wearer's arm from shoulder to elbow and elbow to wrist. Cut two lengths of corrugated cardboard for each arm, making them 2in (50mm) longer than the arm measurements to allow for the overlap at the elbow. Staple the lengths into tube shapes.

9 Slip one corrugated tube inside the other and secure with sticky tape. Make the legs in the same way.

10 Lay out the arms, legs, boots and gloves and spray them all silver.

11 Cut a circle from the bottom of the small cardboard box that will be the head of the robot. This must be large enough to fit over the child's head. Cut some air vents in the sides. Find a clear plastic carton or lid for the visor. Cut a hole the same size out of the head box, push the clear box through and secure with tape.

12 Arrange some egg boxes and paper cups on the box. Mask and spray silver as before. Remove any masking when the paint is dry.

13 Cut holes in the head and body to fit a corrugated tube between them. The holes need to be a tight fit. This part is easier to assemble once the costume is being worn. Add gloves and boots sprayed silver to complete the outfit.

Firework

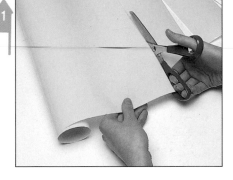

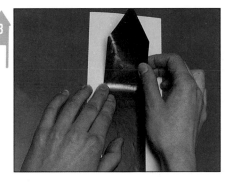

YOU WILL NEED

Red card
White card for templates
Yellow & blue paper
Foil & card for stars
Metallic-finish wrapping paper
Sticky tape & parcel tape
Florists' wire
Oasis florists' foam
Glue & glitter
Aerosol glue
Stapler
Compass
Scissors & craft knife
Elastic
String

☞ This costume is time consuming but not difficult to make.

☞ Replacing the stars and stripes with your own ideas could save some time. You could splash or spray on different coloured paint, for example.

☞ Silver foil wrapped round corrugated cardboard would give a different kind of finish to the rocket.

☞ Aerosol glue must always be used in a very well-ventilated place, preferably outdoors.

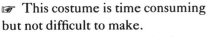

Star template

1 Cut 6 strips of yellow paper 23in × 3½in (584mm × 89mm). Cut 6 strips of blue paper 23in × 2in (584mm × 50mm) and trim one end of each strip to a point.

2 Use the templates to draw and cut out 9 medium blue stars and 11 small silver stars.

3 Glue the yellow strips onto the red card leaving a gap of 4½in (114mm) between them. Glue a blue strip on top of each yellow strip.

4 Add the blue and silver stars.

5 Turn the red card over and reinforce all the sides with strong parcel tape.

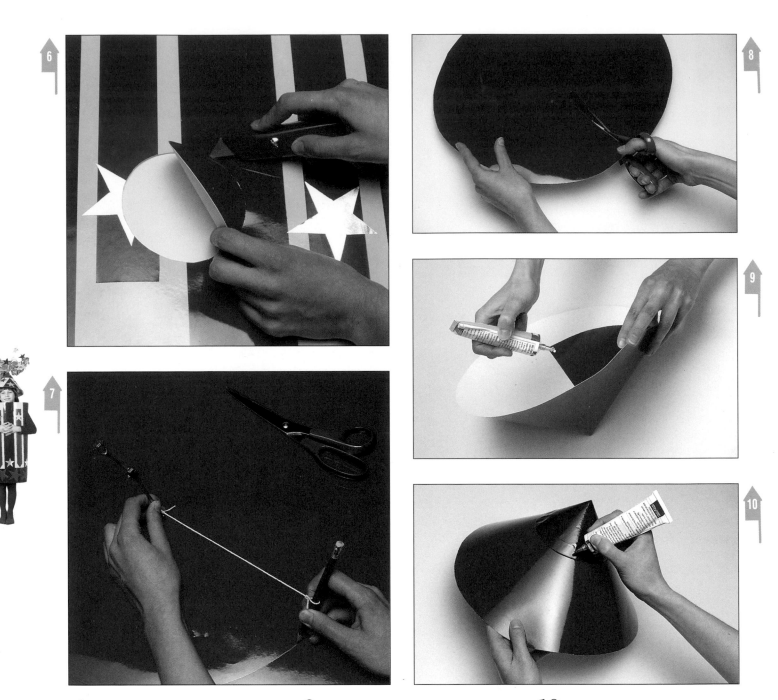

6 Cut two 5in (127mm) diameter holes in the card for arm holes. The edge of each hole should be 3in (76mm) from the top of the card and 9in (228mm) in from the side. The body of the firework is now complete.

7 To make the hat, draw and cut out a 16½in (419mm) diameter circle from red card.

8 Make a cut from the edge of the centre of the circle.

9 Overlap the edges into a cone shape of which the lower edge is 10in (250mm) in diameter and glue the edges securely.

10 Cut a 7in (177mm) circle of blue paper and make a cut from the edge inwards to the centre. Fit the blue cone over the end of the red one and stick firmly into place.

11 Trim a piece of Oasis florists' foam into a cone shape with a blunt knife.

12 Put the foam cone inside the red card cone and stick some tape across to hold it in place.

13 Snip some pieces of metallic paper into a fine fringe. Roll the fringed paper round the end of a piece of florists' wire and secure with sticky tape. You can also decorate pieces of wire with stars.

14 Staple some elastic to the sides of the hat as a chin strap.

15 Push the wires through the top of the hat into the Oasis foam.

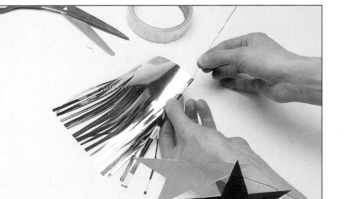

Teapot

YOU WILL NEED

Tracing paper
1 large sheet of polyboard
Gouaches or poster paints &
    brushes
Pencil
Sticky tape & strong tape
Glue
Craft knife
Fabric tape

☞ This costume is very quick and easy to make.

☞ Polyboard is fairly easy to cut with a little practice, but this is probably a job for an adult.

☞ You can adapt almost any pattern and decorative technique for this costume. Polyboard tends to warp a little, so paint both sides.

1 Make the template out of tracing paper and place it on the polyboard. Prick through the tracing with a pin to mark out the outline and patterns. Remove the template and join your pinpricks up with a pencil line. Cut out the teapot shape with a sharp craft knife.

2 Paint the back of the polyboard to prevent warping, then make two ties of fabric tape and attach them with strong tape.

3 Mix some paints to the colours you have chosen and paint the stripes on the front of the teapot.

4 Cut out the hat shape and paint it on both sides.

5 Stick a fabric tape tie onto the back of the hat with strong tape.

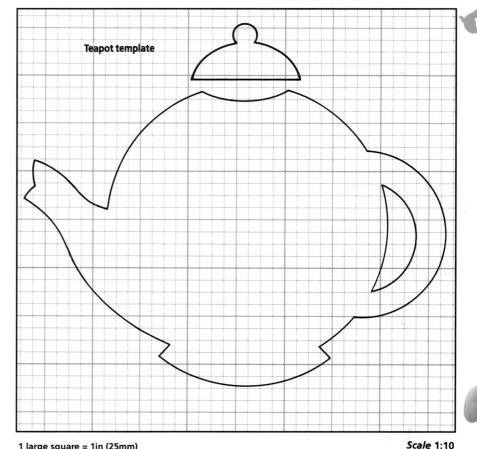

Teapot template

1 large square = 1in (25mm)   *Scale* 1:10

QUICK COSTUME
Pencil

YOU WILL NEED
Paper
Glue
Scissors
Stapler

☞ The basic shape of this quick costume is the same as the Firework but the hat is more pointed.

☞ The body of the pencil is a simple tube. You can cut arm holes as for Firework. Cut the edge of the hat into scallops and colour the point.

5
FOOD

Bag of Sweets 86

Hamburger 92

Picnic 90

Bag of Sweets

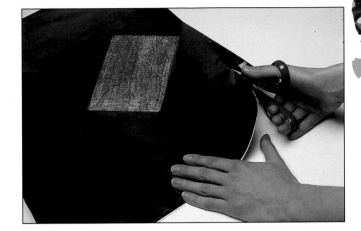

YOU WILL NEED

A selection of boxes
Coloured paper
Coloured cellophane
Sticky tape, strong tape & double-
    sided tape
Elastic
Velcro
Fabric tape
Scissors
Red ribbon

☞ This costume is very cheap and easy to make.

☞ Start collecting boxes of various shapes and sizes well in advance.

☞ Wrap wide cellophane around the wearer and tie at the neck.

1 To cover the round box, cut some cellophane to a generous size.

2 Wrap the box in the cellophane and twist the ends together. Wrap some sticky tape round the twisted cellophane.

3 For the rectangular box, cut some blue paper large enough to cover the box with a little extra at each end.

4 Cut narrow strips of silver paper and stick them to the end of the blue paper. Wrap the box with the blue paper and wrap a wider strip of silver around the centre. Twist up the ends and secure with tape.

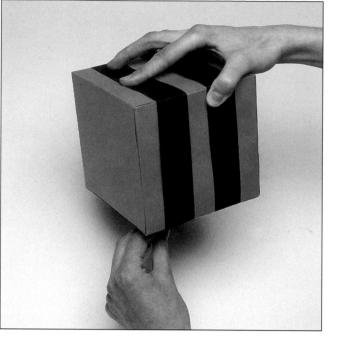

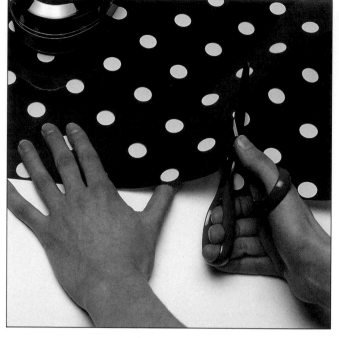

5 Make a liquorice allsort with a square box by covering it with orange paper. Cut some strips of black and white paper. Wrap two strips of black paper around the box, leaving a gap between them.

6 Add a strip of white paper between the black stripes.

7 To make the hat, select an interesting shaped box and cut some spotted wrapping paper to size.

8 Wrap the box and secure with tape. Twist the ends round and secure with more tape.

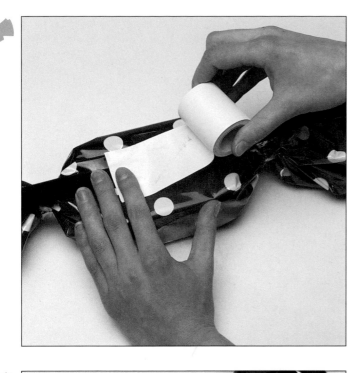

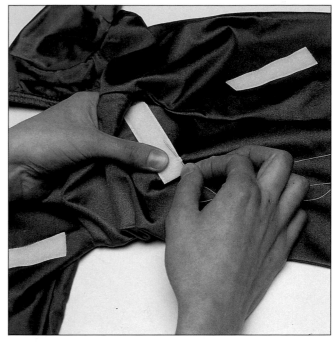

9 Measure enough elastic to go round the back of the head and tie. Attach it to the underside of the hat with strong tape.

10 Stick a piece of velcro onto each sweet.

11 Stick the matching piece of the velcro onto the old leotard or T shirt and arrange the sweets on the costume.

Picnic

YOU WILL NEED

Paper cups, plates & straws
Plastic spoons & knives
Paper jelly moulds
Paper tablecloth
Plastic fruit
Gingerbread men, small fancy
    biscuits & cakes, Bread rolls,
    Cheese (small wrapped portions),
    Crisps . . .
Strong non-toxic glue
Masking tape
Giant sunglasses
Pencil
Scissors

☞ Choose a strong paper tablecloth.
☞ Allow plenty of time for the glue to dry.
☞ Most kitchens will contain enough ingredients for a super picnic!

1 Fold the paper tablecloth in half diagonally. Draw round a plate and cut the neckline. Cut a 12in (304mm) slit in the back to enable the costume to be put on easily. Turn the tablecloth over and reinforce the edge of the neckline with tape. reinforce the edge of the neckline with masking tape.

2 Glue the food and cutlery to the plates. Allow time for the glue to dry.

3 Arrange all the picnic items on the tablecloth and stick firmly in place.

4 Stick small biscuits along the top edge of the giant glasses.

Hamburger

YOU WILL NEED

A circle of foam 25in (635mm) in
    diameter × 2½in (63mm) thick
Polyester wadding
Foam glue
Wax crayons
Stretch jersey cotton
Stockinette
Polyboard or stiff card
Green tissue paper
Fabric tape for straps
Pencil
Paints & paint brush
Scissors & craft knife

☞ This project needs special foam glue, which can usually be bought from the foam suppliers. The gluing is a job for an adult.

☞ The polyester wadding and the stretch jersey cotton are usually available from department stores with dress-fabric sections.

☞ The version shown here is just the front of the burger. A back could easily be made in the same way, but without all the garnishes.

☞ This costume is suitable for an older child (aged 7–12) with some help from an adult.

1 Cut 3 circles of wadding, 17in (431mm), 14in (355mm) and 11in (279mm) in diameter.

2 Stick the largest piece onto the foam, followed by the other two pieces in descending size order. Let the glue dry thoroughly between each piece.

3 Cover the whole thing with the stockinette.

4 Stretch the jersey cotton over the stockinette and glue the edges underneath neatly.

5 Cut out some sesame seed shaped pieces of masking tape and stick them onto the jersey cotton.

6 Colour the whole front of the burger with brown and yellow wax crayon.

7 Cut a piece of card into a bacon-shape and draw on some wavy lines. Paint in the lines roughly in a suitable brown.

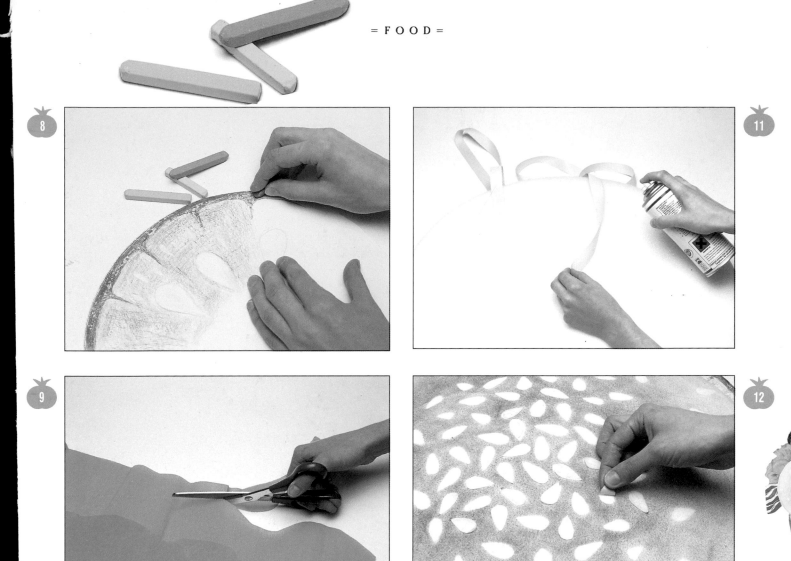

8 Cut out 2 circles of card 12in (304mm) in diameter. Colour one in green as a piece of cucumber, and the other in red as a slice of tomato.

9 Cut some tissue paper with a wavy edge.

10 Stretch the edges of the tissue paper and scrunch it up gently to look like a lettuce leaf.

11 Turn the burger over and glue some tapes firmly to the back to act as the straps. They should be long enough to go over the shoulders, cross over at the back and tie around the waist. Spray some glue round the edge of the back of the burger and stick the bacon, cucumber, tomato and lettuce into place so that they stick out slightly.

12 Take off the masking tape sesame seed masks.

Make a back for the burger if you wish, but remember this side has no sesame seeds or garnishes.

Pineapple

YOU WILL NEED

Yellow, brown & green paper
Yellow paint
Card or polyboard
Glue
Fabric tape for straps

☞ This costume uses the same basic principles as the Teapot (see page 82).

☞ Cut out the pineapple shape in polyboard and cover in yellow paper or paint.

☞ Add strips of brown paper in a cross-cross pattern with small brown shapes in between.

☞ The hat can be a semicircle of polyboard covered in leaves cut from green paper.

646.478 D553c
Dickinson, Gill.
Children's costumes : a

X2003

646.478 D553c
Dickinson, Gill.
Children's costumes : a